South American Animals

Toucans

by Mary R. Dunn

Consulting Editor: Gail Saunders-Smith, PhD

Consultant: Anne R. Hobbs
Public Information Specialist
Cornell Lab of Ornithology
Ithaca, New York

CAPSTONE PRESS
a capstone imprint

Pebble Plus is published by Capstone Press,
1710 Roe Crest Drive, North Mankato, Minnesota 56003.
www.capstonepub.com

Books published by Capstone Press are manufactured with paper
containing at least 10 percent post-consumer waste.

Library of Congress Cataloging-in-Publication Data
Dunn, Mary R.
  Toucans / by Mary R. Dunn.
     p. cm.—(Pebble plus. South American animals)
  Includes bibliographical references and index.
  Summary: "Simple text and photographs present toucans, how they look, where they live, and what they do"—
Provided by publisher.
  ISBN 978-1-4296-7590-1 (library binding)
  1. Toucans—Juvenile literature. I. Title. II. Series.
QL696.P57D86 2012
598.7'2—dc23
                                                                          2011027039

Editorial Credits
Katy Kudela, editor; Lori Bye, designer; Svetlana Zhurkin, media researcher; Kathy McColley, production specialist

Photo Credits
Getty Images: Carol Farneti Foster, 15, Stuart Westmorland, 5; National Geographic Stock: Minden Pictures/
Pete Oxford, 19, Roy Toft, 13; Nature Picture Library: Pete Oxford, 17; Photolibrary: Konrad Wothe, 7; Shutterstock:
Eduardo Rivero, 9, Laurent Ruelle, 11, Mircea Bezergheanu, 21, mountainpix, 1, NH, cover

Note to Parents and Teachers

The South American Animals series supports national science standards related to life science.
This book describes and illustrates toucans. The images support early readers in understanding
the text. The repetition of words and phrases helps early readers learn new words. This book
also introduces early readers to subject-specific vocabulary words, which are defined in the
Glossary section. Early readers may need assistance to read some words and to use the Table of
Contents, Glossary, Read More, Internet Sites, and Index sections of the book.

Printed in the United States of America in North Mankato, Minnesota.
102011   006405CGS12

Table of Contents

Noisy Birds

In the treetops, toucans
hop from branch to branch.
Their loud croaks fill the
South American forests.

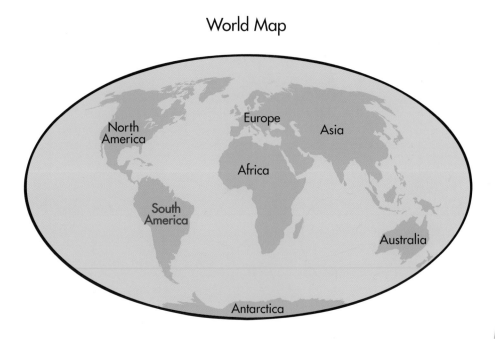

World Map

About 40 kinds of toucans live in Central and South America. During the day, these birds fly in family groups to find food. At night they nest in tree holes.

South America Map

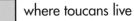 where toucans live

Up Close!

Toucans range in size.
The smallest birds are 11.5
inches (29 centimeters) long.
The largest toucans grow up
to 29 inches (74 cm) long.

Toucans' colorful bills are easy to spot. Their bills are larger than their heads. But looks can be tricky. Toucan bills are lightweight.

Finding Food

With their long bills,

toucans pick fruit from trees.

Sometimes they toss fruit

to each other. Ready? Catch!

Toucans' favorite food is fruit. But they munch on lizards and insects too. They also rob small birds' eggs from nests.

Growing Up

In spring, a female toucan lays up to four white eggs in a nest. Naked, pink-skinned nestlings hatch in about 16 days.

Both parents feed and
take care of their nestlings.
In about 50 days, the young
fly from the nest. Some toucans
live up to 20 years in the wild.

Staying Safe

Adult toucans fly away from eagles, hawks, and jaguars. But toucan eggs and nestlings are helpless. Adults guard their nests from monkeys and snakes.